WHY IT HAPPENED

Donald Gorbach

ISBN-10 197991964X
ISBN-13 978-1979919647

"REMEMBER THE GOOD OLD DAYS WHEN THE BIGGEST PROBLEM OF THE COUNTRY WAS A BJ?"

— ANONYMOUS

www.ingramcontent.com/pod-product-compliance
Lightning Source LLC
Chambersburg PA
CBHW050912260726
48660CB00001B/157